OAK LEAVES

A Circlet of Oak Leaves

The Corona Civica is the highest award for personal bravery in the Eagles – the Roman Army – and the young Auxiliaries find it hard to believe that the lean horse trader Aracos could have won it in his youth. But he did – though the story turns out not to be quite as straightforward as that. Set in second-century Roman Britain this is a story of heroism and courage specially written for younger readers.

Rosemary Sutcliff has written many marvellous novels about Roman Britain, notably *The Eagle of the Ninth*, *The Silver Branch* and *The Lantern Bearers*, and more recently *Frontier Wolf*. No one knows better how to bring to life the contrasts between the civilised life in Roman cities and the bitter fighting which went on on all the frontiers of the Empire to hold back the dark of the encroaching barbarians. *Eagle's Egg*, again written specially for younger readers, is also available in Beavers.

A Circlet of Oak Leaves

Rosemary Sutcliff

Illustrated by Victor Ambrus

Beaver Books

First published in 1965 by
Macmillan and Company Limited
Published in 1968 by
Hamish Hamilton Children's Books Limited
Garden House, 57–59 Long Acre, London WC2E 9J2

This paperback edition published in 1982 by
The Hamlyn Publishing Group Limited
London · New York · Sydney · Toronto
Astronaut House, Feltham, Middlesex, England

ISBN 0 600 20470 7

Printed and bound in Great Britain by
Hazell Watson & Viney Limited, Aylesbury, Bucks
Set in Baskerville

For
all four houses of
Hilsea Modern Girls' School, Portsmouth
(my school)
who adopted me like a battleship or a regimental goat

but just a little bit extra
for Sutcliff House

Contents

Chapter One *11*

Chapter Two *26*

Chapter Three *35*

Chapter Four *44*

Chapter Five *75*

Chapter One

Outside, a little mean spring wind came siffling up from the river, humming across the parade ground of the great fortress in the dark, and tumbling the garbage along the narrow streets of Isca Silurium, but within the open door of the *Rose and Wine Skin* was lamplight and the warmth of braziers, and a companionable rise and fall of voices.

Three young Auxiliary Cavalrymen stood propped against the high trestle table at the far end, talking to the retired Gaulish Javelin man who kept the place, but each with an ear twitching towards the nearest corner, where a knot of Legionaries with long-service bracelets and faces like tanned harness leather, had pulled two benches

together and were setting the world to rights.

'That's what I say!' One of the veterans brought an open hand down on the bench beside him with a slam that set the wine cups jumping. 'All this talk about the need for more Cavalry is so much moon's-milk. It's *us*, the line-of-battle lads that carry the day, every time.'

Another nodded, consideringly. 'It's the speed and mobility they're after, of course.'

And a third laughed into his wine cup. 'Comes in useful for retreating.'

'It was just the same, that time the Picts broke through the Northern Wall – the time the Legate was killed. Six or seven wings of Cavalry, the 6th had with them, when they went up to deal with that lot of blue painted devils, and so far as I can make out the Dacians were the only ones that didn't run like redshanks at the first sound of the Pictish yell.'

The young Auxiliaries had been listening to all this, staring straight before them. Now, one of them, flushing slowly crimson under his ragged cap of barley-pale hair, stepped out from the rest and edged over to the veterans.

'I ask pardon, sir,' he swallowed thickly. 'My mates and I couldn't help hearing. You did say, "As far as you could make out?" You weren't there yourself, then, sir?'

The first veteran looked up, his thick brows shooting towards the roots of his

hair. 'No, I'd a brother there, if it concerns you. He lost a hand when the left flank was crumpled up – it helped him to remember.'

'I'm sorry, sir, but that – losing a hand, I mean – mightn't help him remember very clearly.'

One of the group gave a snort of laughter. 'It's a Cavalry cub. You've hurt his honour, Gavrus.'

'Too bad, Hirpinius,' Gavrus said. 'I've had enough of you, my lad. You're only a little boy, and you don't know anything yet but what the recruiting officer told you. Everyone knows the Tungrians and the Asturians ran like redshanks. Come back and quarrel with me when you've learned to grow a beard!'

There was a roar of laughter from the rest of the Legionaries. The boy's hands clenched into large knuckled red fists. His mates had begun to come up behind him. At any moment there was going to be trouble, and the wine-shop owner looked on anxiously. He had been an Auxiliary himself, and quite clearly, whatever happened, the boys were going to get the sticky end of the vine staff.

But at that moment a rangy, loose-limbed man who had been lounging on the bench nearest the door unfurled himself lazily and came across to join the group.

'The Picts fired the heather, and the flames stampeded the horses.'

Everyone turned to stare at him, including the shop's owner, who knew him well enough: head man to old Lyr the horse breeder, who came down a couple of times a year, with wild-eyed, rough-broken three-year-olds to sell to the garrison horse-master. And the man stared back at them out of slightly widened eyes that seemed pale as rain by contrast with his dark hard-bitten face.

Out of a moment's startled silence, Gavrus said, 'And who in Hades are you?'

'My name is Aracos, for what that's worth; from Thrace in the beginning, from the hills a day's trail westward now!'

'So. And it was fire that stampeded the horses?'

'Yes.'

'You were *there*, I suppose?'

'Yes.'

There was a general gasp, and somebody spluttered into his wine cup.

Then Gavrus, still only half believing, repeated, 'You *were* there?'

'I've lived long enough to be other things before I was a horse breeder.'

'Tungrian Cavalry? or Asturian?'

'Dacian,' Aracos said, and added obligingly, 'the ones who didn't run like redshanks, you know.'

Gavrus took a long swig at his wine, studying him over the rim of the cup all the while, then set it down. 'Oddly enough, I believe you. Just by way of interest, why *didn't* the Dacian horses stampede with the rest?'

'Because the Dacians teach their horses tricks. Haven't you ever seen a Dacian squadron showing off? Standing on horseback or clinging under the brute's belly, or leaping them through the flames of a fire-trench? When the Picts' fire came down on us, our horses were used to the flames, and not afraid.'

The young Auxiliaries looked at each other; one of them whistled under his breath.

'So simple as that, eh?' Abruptly Gavrus shifted along the bench, his leathery face breaking into a grin. 'You've your cup with you – join us and fill up to show there's no ill feeling; you too, my bold infants. Hai, Landlord, more wine all round!' There was a general shifting up to make room, and in a few moments, the Auxiliaries still a little stiff, they were all sitting together, while the shop's owner himself brought the wine.

Pouring the harsh red stuff into the cup Aracos held out, he said, reproachfully, 'It must be four – five times you've been in here, and never said you were one of us.'

'You never asked me,' Aracos said.

Under the warming influence of the wine, the atmosphere was growing friendly, and Aracos felt the warmth of old comradeship and a familiar world drawing him in again, doing more, had he but realised it, than ever the rough Sabine wine could do, to make him unwary. . . .

They talked of girls, the price of barley-beer, the evil-mindedness of Centurions, and so came back again to old battles, to the one particular battle, ten years past.

One of the Legionaries, a dark-faced man more silent than his fellows, looked up abruptly from the depth of his wine cup into which he had been staring. 'Of course! *That* was it!'

'Um?' Gavrus prompted.

'There was something else about that fight – I was trying to remember what it was.'

'And what was it?'

'One of the Auxiliaries earned himself the Corona Civica.'

'Sa ha! 'Tisn't often *that* goes to an Auxiliary. No offence, 'tisn't often it goes to anybody, come to that. Any idea who it was?'

'One of the fire-eating Dacians. I've an idea it was the pennant-bearer.' Hirpinius turned quickly to the stranger in their midst. 'Fools that we are! Of course you're the one who'd be knowing. . . .' He checked, his eyes suddenly widening at what he saw in Aracos's face, his mouth ajar.

But it was one of the Auxiliaries who said in a tone of awed discovery, 'It was you, wasn't it?'

The Corona Civica, the highest award for personal bravery under the Eagles!

They were all staring at him now. 'You?' someone said incredulously. 'You!'

Something flickered far behind the horse breeder's eyes. For a moment he hesitated, then shrugged. 'You could say I earned it – yes.' There was a note of bitter amusement in his tone, as though he laughed inwardly at an ugly jest against himself.

'But man! Why keep it under your helmet! It isn't exactly a thing to be ashamed of!'

'I've no especial reason to talk about it.'

'No reason— Oh, come on, lad, don't pretend you're not human.'

'See now,' Aracos said, 'I'm out from under the Eagles' Wings, and all that is in the past. A circle of gilt oak leaves doesn't carry any weight in the hill horse-runs. Let's drop it.'

But Gavrus, who seemed the leader among the rest, was already shouting for more wine to celebrate, and one of the Auxiliaries, who had been gazing worshipfully at the unsuspected hero in their midst, leaned forward and said, 'Sir – will you tell us about it?'

Aracos's face was flushed, and his pale eyes had reckless sparks in them, but at the eager words he set down his empty wine cup, which the moment before he had been holding up to be refilled with the rest, laughed, and shook his head, and lounged a little unsteadily to his feet. 'Maybe another time – another year. Not tonight; I've an early start for the hills in the morning.'

Making his somewhat zigzag way back to the leather merchant's house on the outskirts of the town where he always lodged when he brought the horses down, Aracos cursed inwardly by all the gods he knew.

What a fool he had been to get caught up in the thing at all. He must have been drunker than he realised. But in his inmost places he knew that drunk or sober would have made little difference. He couldn't have sat there and let the boys take up the challenge alone and land themselves in the trouble they were heading for. Yes, but he might at least have had enough wits about him, when the Corona

Civica came up, not to let the old story show all over his face. Ah well, it would be half a year before his next trip down from the hills; he'd probably never see tonight's bunch again, and old Sylvanus who kept the wine shop would forget.

Chapter Two

But old Sylvanus did not forget. It made too good a story to tell to customers. Finally Aracos simply shrugged and accepted the situation. Being a hero was always good for a free drink, anyway.

He went on accepting it for two and a half years, and then one autumn day he went down to Isca Silurium with the usual string of remounts, struck his bargain with the garrison horse-master, and took himself to the *Rose and Wine Skin* to wash the dust of the horse-yards out of his throat.

Most of the men crowded about the braziers were strangers to him, but two or three Legionaries whom he knew were grouped together in the far corner. He headed across to join them, but mid-way, a voice exploded in his ear.

'Aracos! Now by Jupiter's Thunderbolt, if it isn't Aracos!' And as he looked round, somebody surged into his path; he saw a lean and beaky face with small bright eyes and a coarse, good-humoured mouth, and remembered it from a long time ago.

He felt as though someone had jolted him in the pit of the stomach. 'Nasik! What do you do here?' The words sounded stupid in his own ears.

'What should I be doing here? The Third Wing's just posted here – back from Pannonia. What do you do here?'

'Work for a Horse-Chieftain in the hills. Want any remounts?'

A couple of the older Cavalrymen joined in, grinning and exclaiming at the smallness of the Empire; the younger ones were new since his time. He had a choking desire to turn and thrust his way out into the street again, but that would not stop the thing happening, only mean it happening behind his back. . . .

And then old Sylvanus joined his voice to the rest. 'Here's a fine reunion.

You'll have been together in that northern fighting, ten years ago? Well now, you're just the lads we want, for we've never yet got him to tell us how he came by the Corona Civica.'

A couple of the Legionaries whom Aracos knew, had joined the group and added their voices to the rest. 'Now *you* can tell us. Come on now, tell the tale; don't be bashful, my wood anemone!'

Nasik looked from them to Aracos, puzzled; then burst into a shout of laughter. 'Corona Civica? It's a jest, isn't it?'

There was a sudden uneasiness among the onlookers, a sharp, startled pause. 'A jest? No, why should it be?' someone said.

Nasik broke off his laughter. 'You *don't* mean to say – did he tell you he got the Civica?'

Aracos stood quite still, fronting the perplexed and startled faces. There was a little smile on his mouth, as set as though it were carved in stone.

One of the Legionaries, as though defending himself in advance from the

charge of being easily duped, said, 'One of the Dacians *did* get the Civica in that fight.'

'Yes, but not this one. Why, by our Lady of the Foals! He's never been a soldier! He was a medical orderly – an Army butcher's fetch-and-carry man!'

A second Dacian had come up beside the first. 'So you thought you'd snap up Felix's cast-off glory, did you? He being dead and not needing it any more!'

The wine-shop owner turned a troubled eye on the silent man in their midst. 'Well? You'd best be saying something, hadn't you?'

The whole shop was silent to hear his answer, and Aracos, looking round at them with that lazy smile still engraved on his lips, saw that they were not exactly hostile – yet – but the startled perplexity was hardening into disgust, and a hint of the delight of boys watching a cat with a pannikin tied to its tail.

'Surely. It's all perfectly true,' he said on a note of amusement.

'But why?' – the wine-shop keeper began.

Aracos shrugged. 'It's dull, up in the hills. I wanted to see if you would be fools enough to believe me – and behold, you were.'

A growl of anger answered him, and a small red-haired Legionary got menacingly to his feet. 'Why you – you – I'll teach you to make fools of us again!'

But his neighbour seized him by the shoulder and slammed him back on to the bench. 'Leave him be. He's not worth getting rounded up by the Watch Patrol for, he looks a much worse fool than we do, anyway.'

Aracos turned to the landlord. 'I came in for a drink, but I don't much care for the smell in here tonight.' He turned, and pushed out into the windy dark, careful not to betray by the set of his shoulders that he heard the shout of laughter and the insults that followed him.

One man among the Dacians had looked up with a start when Nasik first shouted the newcomer's name, and had remained quite still, watching him, through the whole ugly scene that came after. In the somewhat shamefaced silence that followed the laughter, before the shout went up for more wine, he got up with some excuse to his companions, and left the wine shop.

Outside in the street he checked a moment, then turned uphill towards the Dexter Gate of the fortress, still dimly visible in the gusty autumn twilight.

Aracos went downhill towards his lodging. He would not think until he got back to the little room under the roof where he could be alone. He must get away from people, from faces in the light of open doorways.

He came to the leather merchant's door and went in. The daughter of the house came out from an inner room when she heard him; he had always liked her, but tonight he only wanted to be left alone. 'You are early,' she said, 'but supper will be ready soon.'

He shook his head. 'I am not hungry, Cordaella.'

He went past her, up the ladder to the room under the roof. He kicked the door shut behind him, and sat down on the narrow cot. The small earthenware lamp had been lit ready for him, early though he was, and he sat staring at it, not seeing it at all, seeing only the faces in the *Rose and Wine Skin*, hearing the laughter. He wouldn't come down to Isca Silurium again. Old Lyr could make some other arrangement about getting his horses sold. The small sharp pain that came on him sometimes after an especially hard struggle with an unbroken colt, was flickering under his ribs and down his left arm, but he was no more aware of it than he was of the lamp flame.

Chapter Three

A long while later, feet came up the ladder, and a hand was on the latch. Cordaella's voice said, 'Aracos.'

'Go away, Cordaella. I'm not hungry.'

'There is someone here to speak with you.'

'Tell whoever it is,' Aracos said carefully and distinctly, 'to go to Gehenna!'

There was a murmur of voices. The latch rattled down, the door opened and closed again. 'I am sorry,' said a quiet voice. 'Don't blame the woman; she tried to stop me.'

Aracos swung round to see a slight, youngish man with the badge of the Dacian Horse on his belt buckle, and on the breast of his tunic the entwined serpents of Esculapius that marked him for one of the Medical Corps. Aracos had not consciously noticed him in the wine shop, but he knew him again.

'Get out!'

'Presently.'

'Now! Didn't you have enough fun in the *Rose and Wine Skin* that you must come after me for more?'

'I would have been here sooner.' The young Medic ignored that. 'But had to go back to my quarters to fetch this that I have for you – from Felix.'

'Felix is dead,' Aracos said dully. 'I didn't know, until they said so this evening.'

'He died between my hands, two years ago in Pannonia. He bade me take this, and get it to a certain Aracos from Thrace, who was a medical orderly with the Dacians during the Pictish troubles. But you had left the Eagles, and I could not pick up your trail, so I have kept it with my own gear ever since, just on the chance. . . .' He bent and laid on the cot a flat bundle wrapped in a piece of old uniform cloth. 'The Empire is a small place, as our friends said.'

Aracos took up the bundle and slowly folded back the tattered cloth. Inside was a battered circlet of gilded bronze fashioned into the form of oak leaves. The Corona Civica!

'He said it was yours by rights.'

Aracos was silent a few moments, holding the thing gently between his hands. 'How did he die?'

'Of wounds taken in driving off an attack on the supply train he was escorting. It was three days later, before he got them into camp. The Gods know how he kept going so long.'

In the silence the wind gusted against the house, and sent a rustling charge of dry leaves along the court outside.

'I had a feeling,' the young Medic said at last, 'that you could have said something in your own defence, tonight, and that you deliberately chose to hold it back.'

'Did you?' Aracos said, without interest.

He was remembering how it had all begun, the day when he had gone down from his village in the Rhodope Mountains with two other lads, to the recruiting station at Abdera. He could sit a horse with anyone, and it had not occurred to him that the small sharp pain that sometimes caught him in the chest after running uphill was anything to keep him out of the Thracian Cavalry. At Abdera a man with entwined serpents on the breast of his tunic had made each of them in turn run to the sacred olive tree half a mile away and back without stopping, and then laid his ear against their chests and listened to something inside. The other two had been accepted, but not Aracos, though he had run faster than either of them. He wondered later if the man had heard the small pain in his chest that the running had given him.

He hadn't gone home, he would have been shamed, but he found that there was room for other men than warriors under the Eagles, jobs for which you did not have to have anyone listening to your chest. He had liked the man with the entwined serpents, and he was interested by this running and listening; he wanted to know what you could hear inside people that told you they had a pain. And so he had become a medical orderly, with the Thracians at first, then with the Dacian Horse in the far-off province of Britain.

He remembered the great outpost fort of Trimontum on the skirts of its three-peaked hill. He remembered Felix at Cavalry manoeuvres, Felix in his pennant-bearer's wolfskin, riding full tilt at the head of the flying squadron, with the long sleeve-pennant of scarlet silk filling with the wind and streaming from its silver serpent-head on the lance point. It was just at the end of those manoeuvres that the youngster had been thrown and broken his collar bone; but for that they would probably never have even spoken to each other, for clerks and orderlies and such,

Aracos had very soon discovered, were in the Legions and Auxiliaries, but not *of* them. The odd thing was that they were very much alike save that Felix was not so dark, so that for all the seven or eight years difference between them, old Diomedes the camp surgeon called them Castor and Pollux, when Felix came to have his shoulder tended.

He remembered news of unrest filtering down from the north at the end of a long dry summer, the smoke signals feathering the sky; the Dacian Wings under those slim scarlet serpent pennants riding out to join the 6th Legion on its forced march northward. He remembered following with the baggage carts in the dust of the marching columns, the heather swimming in the heat, the Pictish harrying that began on the second day; a wolf-pack worrying along their flanks, nightly attacks, scouting patrols that came back bloody and at half strength – one that never came back at all.

He remembered the last night, the

knowledge on them all that full battle was coming with the morning; the ordered stir of the camp that never died down all through the tense hours of darkness.

Chapter Four

In the first ghost-grey light before a misty dawn, Aracos went down to the latrine trenches beyond the horse lines (the Legions never camped a night without digging such trenches and setting up a stockade) and found Felix there, his wolfskin flung behind him, being violently sick.

'Felix! What is it?'

And then as the boy crouched back on his heels and turned a sweat-streaked face to him, he knew. Felix's squadron had run into trouble more than once during the forced march north, and lost several men; the last time, he had got back with a friend's body slung across his horse's withers, a body with part of the face carried away by a throw-spear, that had still been alive when they set

out on the struggle back to camp. That had been once too often.

'Aracos!' The boy was shaking from head to foot, and his teeth chattered as though he had fever. 'Aracos! Thank the Gods it's you! Help me—'

Aracos caught his shoulders to steady him. 'You're the only one who can do that.'

'*You* can – you *can*.'

'How?'

'There must be something. The German Berserks chew leaves of some sort, don't they?' He was beyond shame; that would come later. 'I'd get drunk, but it only makes me sleepy.' He bent his face into his hands.

'Stop it!' Aracos said. 'You can! I've known men as sick as a cat in the dawn and fight like tigers an hour later.'

But when the other looked up again, he knew that he was wrong; he had served with the Eagles long enough to know the look on the face of a man who had reached the end of what he could take. Now, what in the name of Night's Daughters was to be done? Whatever it was, it must be done quickly.

Scarcely realising what he did, he caught up the wolfskin and dragged the boy to his feet, and an instant later was crouching with him behind the long mound of earth turned up by the trench diggers. 'Listen – I can't give you anything; I can't and I won't!' Then as Felix made a convulsive movement, 'No, *listen*; there's only one way out – we're about the same size, and like enough to pass in the dust of fighting. Strip off those leathers.'

'You mean you—'

'Yes.' Aracos was already yanking at a shoulder buckle.

'You can't.'

'I've got to, haven't I? Quick now, off with your breeks.' Felix obeyed him, but his eyes had a strange blankness, as though he did not hear. Aracos snatched the breeks from him and dragged them on. 'Where's your horse.'

Felix's gaze turned on him with the same blankness.

'Your horse! Where's he picketed?'

'The end of the second line.'

'Right.' He had the tunic on now, belt, sword belt, the great wolfskin with the head pulled well forward on his brows. 'I'm away now. Don't follow for a hundred heart-beats. Then make for the baggage park, lie up in one of the tilt carts nearest to the stockade until I

come back, and pray to the Gods, for your own sake as well as mine, that I *do* come back. I'll whistle "The Girl I Kissed at Clusium". Don't move until you hear the tune.'

The young pennant-bearer still seemed in a daze, but he could not wait to make sure he understood. All he could do was to take the youngster's place and hope for a miracle to bring them both through the day without disaster.

Looking back, he still did not know whether he had done right, he only knew that at the time there had seemed nothing else that he could do, and that the miracle had happened. In the ordered bustle of the camp, with the watch fires turning sickly and scarcely a finger of light in the sky, he had got through the issue of food, collected the serpent pennant from its place with the Cohort Colours and the Eagle itself before the Legate's tent. He had seen it done so often that he made no obvious mistake in the ceremonial; and at half-light, with morning mist thickening among the hills, found himself riding, still unrecognised, behind the Captain at the head of the two wings of Dacian Horse.

The manoeuvring for position, the coming and going of Scouts, the hurried Councils of War in the Legate's tent, belonged to yesterday, and he had known nothing of them anyway; his business in life was the medical supplies, not the tactics of hill warfare. And now,

as they rode down into the steep river valley across the narrows of which the Tungrians had been standing to all night, and took up their position in reserve behind the steadily forming battle line, his business was with the light sleeve of scarlet silk lifting and stirring from the lance shaft in his hand; to carry out the pennant-bearer's duties with no betraying mistake, and to keep his face hidden.

The rising mist was warm and milky, no freshness in it. The waiting seemed interminable.

And then far ahead, a flurry of shouting broke the silence, and all along the battle line and the ranks of the Reserves ran a tiny ripple of the nerve ends, like an unheard touch on the taut strings of a harp. Somewhere out in front the Roman outposts were already engaged. The shouting came nearer; Pictish war horns were snarling in the mist and the Roman trumpets crowed in answer. And now, to the shouting, was added a clanging and clashing and an earth-shaking

rumble that Aracos had heard before, but never from the fighting-ranks, and out of the mist swept a column of war chariots, driven and manned by naked, blue-painted warriors.

They swept across the Roman front, raining down throw-spears which the

Legionaries caught for the most part on their shields, and wheeling about on the steepening skirts of the hillside, would have cut in between the first rank and the second. But the Cretan archers posted between the Asturian squadrons on the left flank, wheeled half left as they passed, and loosed a flight of short arrows into their midst, aiming for the teams rather than the men. Team after team came down in kicking chaos and a rending crash of broken yoke-poles and torn-off wheels; the charge lost shape and impetus, and swung away, straightening itself back into some kind of order as it went; and from farther to the right, another column came screaming down upon the Roman battle line. The mist was growing ragged before the light breeze that had begun to wake with the dawn, and a brief gleam of light from the rising sun slid into the eyes of the archers on the right wing, making their aim less sure; a team went down here and there, but the wild head of the column was into the Tungrian Cavalry before they could be stopped, and in the same instant, from dead ahead, a wave of foot-warriors came yelling out of the mist and flung themselves upon the pilums of the main battle line. The pilums drank blood, but there seemed always more, where the first wave had come from.

Aracos, in his place in the Reserve, the slim scarlet banner hanging limp from the lance-shaft in his hand, was never clear about what happened then. All that his mind kept of the battle, afterwards, was a memory of roaring chaos, until suddenly, unbelievably, the trumpets were sounding for Advance and Follow-Up, and he realised with a leap of the heart, that the Picts were falling back.

The whole struggle was moving north-westward up the curve of the valley. Close beside him, the Dacian Captain snapped an order, and the Cavalry trumpets were yelping. Felix's horse as though catching the surge of excitement, flung up his head with a shrill squeal, and buckled forward under his new rider. But it was not yet fighting time for the Reserves. They only moved forward, keeping station behind the reeling battle line, over dead and wounded men.

The northward surge of the battle slowed and checked once, as though the

Picts were making a desperate stand, then rolled on again. The valley swung farther west, rising underfoot, the mist was growing more and more ragged, and suddenly it rolled away like a curtain, still clinging to the northern side of the valley but leaving clear the sheer heather slopes to the south, where a great spur of rock and scree jutted out almost to overhang the narrowing glen.

The man beside him shouted, 'Mithras! Look up there!' and following his wildly pointing finger, Aracos saw the crest of the spur swarming with Painted Men. They were prising loose stones out of the heather, and at that very instant the first of these, flung by a naked giant, came whizzing down with the power of a ballista bolt, and somewhere among the surging mass of Legionaries a man screamed – half a scream. But a far worse menace was the great boulder, already perilously poised, that topped the crag, round which the Painted Men were labouring with deadly purpose. There were lesser stones

to be hauled from about its base, and spear butts made flimsy levers for shifting such a huge mass, but Aracos saw with a sickening lurch of the heart that it was only a matter of time before that vast boulder came crashing down into the midst of the Roman battlemass, bringing with it, by the look of things, half the hillside as it came.

The Eagles had been led into a trap!

Ahead, the Legionary trumpets were sounding, fiercely urgent. They were echoed by the light notes of the Cavalry trumpets, and three squadrons of Asturians broke away and headed at a slant up the steep hillside, while below them the Centurions fought to get the Cohorts back from the deadly menace of the rock-crowned spur and the great stones already crashing down, and the Pictish warrior-swarm fought as desperately to pen them in.

Suddenly, out of the low sunlight leapt flame that danced up just below the hill shoulder, and spread from point to point into a single curved line of fire, red in the daylight, rippling and undulating towards the horsemen.

'Gods! They've fired the heather!'

In the face of the fire across their path, the Asturians' horses balked and wheeled about, snorting in terror, and flung back from the flames, those in front spreading instant confusion among those behind, and the whole lot, for all the efforts of their riders to check and turn them, stampeding away downhill like unbroken colts. And now the horses on the battle-wings were catching the smell of the fire and the terror of their own kind, flinging this way and that. A few moments more and they would be utterly unmanageable.

'Right! It's us now!' The Dacian Captain gave quick orders to his message-rider: 'Get back to the Decurian Sextus and bid him take Second Wing and the hind four squadrons of First forward to hold the battle flank. The rest of First Wing— *With Me*!'

Trumpets yelped again. Aracos drove his heel into the bay's flank and was

away at the Captain's side; the wind of their going took the thin scarlet silk and the body of the serpent pennant filled and rippled out, as he set his horse at the slope, the rest drumming at their heels. Smoke wafted into his eyes, sparks and wisps of burning heather were breaking free and drifting ahead of the main blaze, little red tongues licking up wherever they landed; the thin wall of fire, leaping high now in the morning breeze, rippled like the thin red serpent silk, bending over as though to greet and engulf them. Aracos felt the bay brace and gather himself under him, then hold straight on, no swerving from the flames ahead. Let the Tungrians laugh in future at the Dacians' tricks!

At the last instant the Captain gave a great shout, then with his cloak flung across nose and mouth, plunged straight into the wall of flame. Aracos galloped at his side, face driven down into the wolfskin. Hideous, blasting heat lapped him round, not a wall of flame but a whole world of flame. He choked into

the wolfskin as pain tore at his eyes and throat and lungs – then they were through. There was a stink of singeing horsehide, sparks hung in the rough wolfskin and in the horse's mane, a fringe of flame lengthened the tail of the scarlet serpent. Ahead, the blackened and smoking hillside rose to the spur where the Painted Men still laboured savagely about the great tottering

boulder. But away to the right, something moved under cover of the smitch, and next instant a flurry of javelins and sling-stones took the Dacians on the flank. Men and horses went down. Still riding hard for the spur, Aracos was aware of the Captain swaying beside him, clutching at the shaft of a javelin that stuck out from under his collarbone – choking to him a last order to take them on and clear the spur, before he pitched down among the horses' hooves.

So he took them on, through a vicious squall of slingstones. Where the ground grew too steep to ride they dropped from the horses and ran on, crouching with heads down behind their light bronze-rimmed bucklers. By the time they reached the spur, hearts and lungs bursting within them, he had no idea how many or how few were still behind him; he had had no chance to look round. He did not even know that many of the horses, lightened of their riders' weight, had come scrambling after them, bringing their own weapons, the stallions' weapons of teeth and trampling hooves, into the fight. He only knew that the time came when there were no more Painted Men left alive on the spur, and that the terrible boulder, swaying as it seemed to every breath, was still there.

They jammed loose stones under it, and added a few war-painted bodies for good measure, but to Aracos it was all

hazy, and the only thing that seemed quite real was the pain in his chest that spread all down his shield-arm and made a buzzing darkness before his eyes. He fought the darkness off. If he collapsed now they would pull off the wolfskin to find where he was wounded, and see his face. But he never afterwards had the least idea how they got back to the main force, nor how the rest of that day went, save that somehow, incredibly, it ended in a Roman victory, dragged out of what had nearly been the most hideous defeat.

When things began to seem real again, he was back in camp, and tending Felix's bay, who had a spear gash in his flank and looked, like his neighbours in the picket lines, to have been ridden hard all day. There was a vague half-memory in him of having been hunting – not deer or wild ox, but painted men among the heather; and a rather clearer one of setting a wisp of scorched scarlet silk on a lance shaft back in the row of Colours before the Legate's tent.

In the dusk and the ordered confusion, it was not hard to slip away unnoticed, but it could not be long before the cry went up for the pennant-bearer of the Dacian Horse. With the wolfskin stripped off and rolled into an unbetraying bundle under one arm, he made for the baggage park, and slipped in among the carts nearest to the stockade. The pain in his chest came and went, like a beast flexing its muscles to spring. He leaned against a wheel, and whistled softly, as well as he could for lack of breath, the first bars of 'The Girl I Kissed at Clusium'.

There was no answering whistle, but as he listened, something stirred in the next cart. He went to it quickly, and pulling himself up, peered under the tilt.

'Felix!'

Among the sacks and bales, something stirred again, and the pale blur of a face swam in the gloom. 'All's over,' he whispered, 'and all's well. Out now – they'll be missing you at any moment.'

'Aracos! Oh, thank the Gods you're back! I was – so afraid you would go down.'

'For your sake, or mine?' Aracos said grimly, and then, 'Na, forget I said it. Get these on and out with you and take over your empty place. They've killed the Captain. Remember you led First Wing up to clear the Painted People from a hill spur where they were heaving rocks down on the Legion. They fired the heather, but you got through. There's a singed place on the flank of the wolfskin, you'd best rub your face in it.'

He was dragging off the leather breeks as he spoke, and tossed them into the cart after tunic and wolfskin. He heard an inarticulate sound that was almost a sob. The boy had lain there all day long, alone with himself, and the Mother of Foals alone knew what kind of shape he was in now, to carry the thing through; but he could not wait to see. The beast in his chest was getting ready to spring, and he must get clear of the baggage park while he could.

There was a high sweet ringing in his ears, and black webs spun between his eyes and the camp fires, as he turned away towards the wattle shelters beyond a knot of hawthorn scrub where the Medics would be busy with the wounded. He must have been missed, of course; he must think of some reason to give, some story to tell that would not turn anyone's thoughts towards the Dacians' pennant-bearer. . . . He was quite close to one of the fires when the beast in his chest leapt.

He took one more step, choking for air against the rending teeth and claws, and had just sense and time left to turn towards the fire as he stumbled to his knees. The black webs spun into solid darkness as he sank forward on to his face among the hot ash. His last thought was that at least the marks of fire on him would be accounted for.

When the darkness ebbed again, he was lying on his back with men standing round him, and one kneeling over him with an ear pressed to his chest, just as the man had done who turned him down for the Thracian Horse.

'He just loomed up out of the darkness and went head first into the fire,' someone said. 'Has he been at the barley spirit?'

'No,' said the man with an ear to his chest, and the voice was that of Diomedes, the surgeon. Then, straightening up, 'Poor brute, he must have felt it coming on him and hidden away like a sick animal.'

Another voice pointed out, 'You heard

what these men said; he hasn't just been lying around here all day, sir.'

'I said hidden away, not lying around. I imagine he thought the worst was over, and was on his way back to duty when it took him again.'

In the end, they had decided that he had some sort of rift in his heart that the strain of the campaign had worsened, and he was invalided out with a small sickness gratuity, just about the time the news came through that Felix had won the Corona Civica for clearing the Picts from the hill spur after the Wing Captain was killed, and thereby most likely saving the Legion.

They had been back at Trimontum leaving the north quiet behind them, a good while by then, and Aracos was going south next day with a returning supply train; south, and out from the service of the Eagles.

Felix had hunted him out, where he had gone down the river glen to make a last small sacrifice at the Altar to Fortune which one of the garrison had put up long ago. The boy looked old and haggard, as though he were the one who had been ill. 'I cannot go through with this!' he said desperately.

'Yes, you can.'

'I *can't*! I'm going to tell them. I don't care what they do to me, anything would be better than this!'

And Aracos had caught him by the shoulders as he had done once before. 'Now listen! The Gods know why I was fool enough to do what I did for you, but this I know; you're not going to undo it all now!'

There had been a long silence, broken only by the voice of the little stream that flowed out from under the shrine, and then Felix had moaned softly, like something with a physical hurt. 'I could hack myself to pieces! I don't know what happened and I don't know it won't happen again. . . . If only I could be the one to pay. . . .'

Aracos had tightened his grip. 'You'll pay your share, all right. All your life

you're going to have to wear that circlet of gilded oak leaves through your shoulder-strap, and feel men's eyes on it, and know the truth behind it. Oh, you'll pay, Felix, so we can cry quits.'

And he had seen the slack despairing lines of the boy's face tauten, and his head go up, as he took the strain.

'But what will you do?' he asked after a while.

'Stay on in Britain. I spent my first year in the province on garrison duty at Burrium. There's good horse country among the Welsh hills. I might try to get work there. I've my gratuity; I shan't starve while I'm looking for it.'

Chapter Five

A whirling moth blundered into the lamp flame, and fell away, singed and sodden, and Aracos was in the present again. He was alone, though he had not heard the young Medic go, and still holding between his hands the battered circlet of gilded oak leaves. In one place the bronze showed through, where the gilt was all rubbed away by the shoulder-strap through which it had been worn for more than eight years.

Again he remembered Felix's set face. Oh yes, Felix had paid his price. And in the end – what had the Medic said? 'He died between my hands, two years ago in Pannonia . . . of wounds taken in driving off an attack on the supply train he was escorting. It was three days later, before he got them into

camp. The Gods know how he kept going so long.'

A small inward bitterness that had been with Aracos for ten years suddenly fell away. He had been worth saving, that boy. He thought with a detached interest, as though it concerned somebody else and not himself at all, that now he could tell the truth, and be believed. But the thought remained detached. One didn't betray a friend merely because he was dead.

But he knew, for no very clear reason, that because that wild day's work ten years ago had not been wasted, because Felix had died in the way he had done, and dying, had sent him the battered circlet of oak leaves, he would bring down the remounts again next spring, and go to the *Rose and Wine Skin* again – and again – and again, until the story grew too threadbare to be bothered with any more, and he had come out beyond it.

He folded the Corona Civica carefully in its bit of old cloth again, and getting up, opened the door and called down the ladder, 'Cordaella! Is there any supper left?'

More Beaver Books

We hope you have enjoyed this Beaver Book. Here are some of the other titles:

Eagle's Egg An exciting story about a young standard-bearer in Roman Britain, who earns his promotion – and the right to marry the girl he loves – in a surprising way. Specially written for younger readers by Rosemary Sutcliff, and strikingly illustrated by Victor Ambrus

The Mother Goose Book Beautifully illustrated in delicate colours by Alice and Martin Provensen, this book of nursery rhymes is ideal for younger readers or for reading aloud

The Sea Witch Meg is sure that she and her little brother Maxie can manage on their own for a couple of days. But they quarrel on the beach and Maxie disappears – suppose he has drowned? Panic-stricken, Meg rushes for help to their neighbour, a lady they had always thought was a witch. . . . An exciting thriller for younger readers by Joan G. Robinson

These and many other Beavers are available from your local bookshop or newsagent, or can be ordered direct from: Hamlyn Paperback Cash Sales, PO Box 11, Falmouth, Cornwall TR10 9EN. Send a cheque or postal order made payable to the Hamlyn Publishing Group, for the price of the book plus postage at the following rates:
UK: 40p for the first book, 18p for the second book, and 13p for each additional book ordered to a maximum charge of £1.49;
BFPO and Eire: 40p for the first book, 18p for the second book, plus 13p per copy for the next 7 books and thereafter 7p per book;
OVERSEAS: 60p for the first book and 18p for each extra book.

New Beavers are published every month and if you would like the *Beaver Bulletin*, a newsletter which tells you about new books and gives a complete list of titles and prices, send a large stamped addressed envelope to:

Beaver Bulletin
The Hamlyn Group
Astronaut House
Feltham
Middlesex TW14 9AR

204707